WITHDRAWN

Awful, Disgusting Parasites

TAPE-WORMS

BARBARA CILETTI

🌐 WORLD BOOK

BOLT

This World Book edition of *Tapeworms*
is published by agreement between
Black Rabbit Books and World Book, Inc.
© 2017 Black Rabbit Books,
2140 Howard Dr. West,
North Mankato, MN 56003 U.S.A.
World Book, Inc.,
180 North LaSalle St., Suite 900,
Chicago, IL 60601 U.S.A.

Design and Production by Michael Sellner
Photo Research by Rhonda Milbrett

Library of Congress Control Number: 2015954685

HC ISBN: 978-0-7166-9785-5   PB ISBN: 978-0-7166-9786-2

Printed in the United States at CG Book Printers,
North Mankato, Minnesota, 56003. PO #1792 4/16

Image Credits

Contents

CHAPTER 1

Unexpected Ingredient

A man took a bite of his beef supper. He saw it was a little undercooked. But he didn't worry about it. What he didn't know was that creatures were hiding in his food. He had just eaten baby tapeworms.

Worms in the Body

Inside the man's body, tapeworm **parasites** grew into adults. Parasites live and feed on people and other animals. These worms used the man's body to grow and lay eggs. And it all happened without him even knowing.

Tapeworm Parts

EACH **SEGMENT** PRODUCES EGGS

SUCKER

NECK

HOOK

Tapeworm Symptoms

Tapeworms don't usually cause **symptoms**. But sometimes, people have clues that tapeworms are in them.

WEIGHT LOSS

WORM PARTS IN POOP

TIRED FEELING

VOMITING

UPSET
STOMACH

9

CHAPTER 2

Tricky Travelers

Tapeworms are flat worms that live inside people. They hook onto a person's **intestines** and eat partly **digested** food. As they grow, they begin to make eggs.

These worms can be 50 feet (15 meters) long.

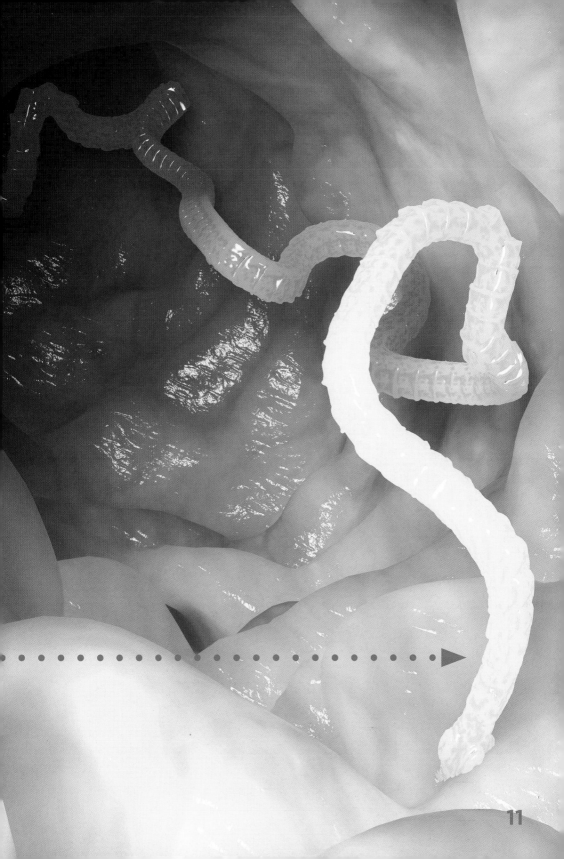

In the Waste

Inside a person, the eggs travel through the intestines. They leave the person's body along with his or her poop.

In some parts of the world, people don't have good bathrooms. They poop and pee on the ground. Animals, such as pigs or cows, eat the waste. And they eat the tapeworm eggs too.

Growing

Inside a cow or pig, the eggs hatch. The baby tapeworms are called larvae. Larvae travel through the animal in its blood. They land in its muscles and form bubbles called **cysts**. No one knows the larvae are there.

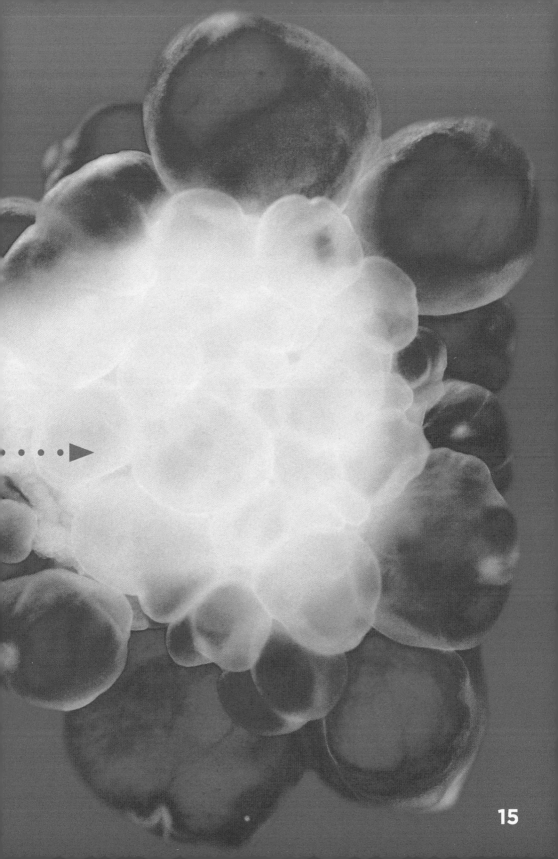

Eating the Worms

When the animals are killed for food, the cysts stay in the meat. Cooking the meat kills the worms. But eating uncooked meat causes trouble. The cysts will grow into adults in a person's body. Then the cycle starts over again.

TAPEWORM LIFE CYCLE

6

Adults make eggs. The eggs leave the human's body through waste.

5

Larvae grow into adults.

4

Humans eat the larvae in uncooked meat.

1
tapeworm eggs

2
Cows or pigs
eat the eggs.

3
Eggs grow into
larvae inside
the animal.

CHAPTER 3

Taking Care of Tapeworms

Tapeworms live all around the world. These parasites spread quickly in places without good waste removal. In these places, animals can eat human waste. The animals pick up tapeworm eggs from the poop. Keeping animals away from waste helps stop the spread.

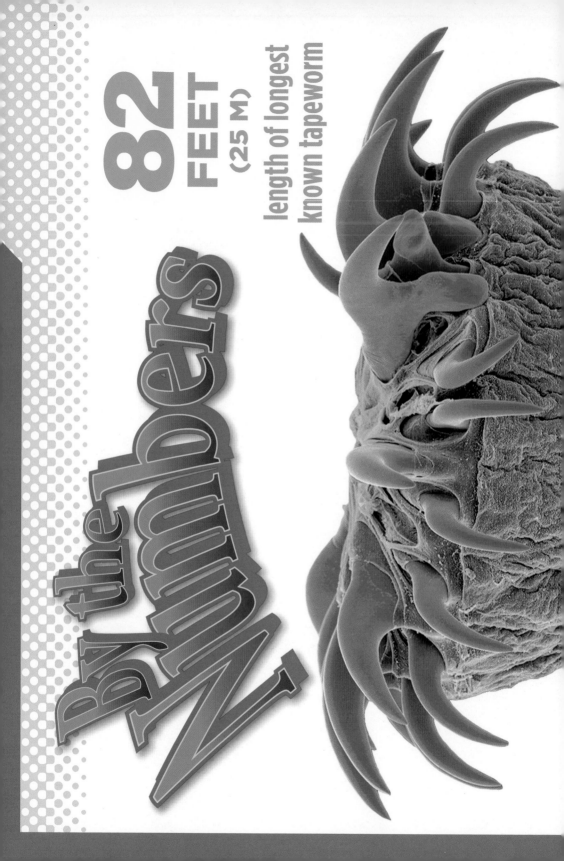

By the Numbers

82 FEET
(25 M)
length of longest
known tapeworm

30

years a tapeworm can live in a person

50,000 people die from tapeworms each year.

500,000 EGGS LAID BY A TAPEWORM EVERY DAY

50 MILLION people get tapeworms every year.

CHAPTER 4

Treatment and Prevention

Avoiding tapeworms is the best way to stop them. But tapeworms affect millions of people every year. Doctors have medicines that help. These medicines kill the parasites.

Tapeworm parasites are troublemakers. But they don't need to be scary. With clean hands and cooked food, people can be worm free!

Stop
Tapeworms

tapeworm

wash hands

cook or freeze meat

Crazy  Tapeworms

Tapeworms are crazy creatures. They can't see. But they can tell light from dark. And did you know dogs and cats get tapeworms too?

Some people eat tapeworms on purpose. They do it to lose weight. But using the worms like this is dangerous. It's also illegal.

avoid (uh-VOYD)—to keep away from

cyst (SIST)—a growth filled with liquid inside the body

digest (dy-JEST)—to change the food eaten into a form that can be used by the body

intestine (en-TE-sten)—the part of the digestive system where most food is digested; it is a long tube made up of the small intestine and the large intestine.

parasite (PAR-uh-syt)—a plant or animal that lives in or on another plant or animal and gets its food or protection from it

segment (SEG-ment)—one of the parts into which something can be divided

symptom (SYMP-tuhm)—a change in the mind or body that means a disease is present

BOOKS

Cusick, Dawn. *Get the Scoop on Animal Poop: From Lions to Tapeworms, 251 Cool Facts about Scat, Frass, Dung, and More*. Watertown, MA: Imagine Pub., 2012.

Kawa, Katie. *Tapeworms*. Freaky Freeloaders: Bugs that Feed on People. New York: PowerKids Press, 2015.

Terry, Paul. *Top 10 Deadly Animals: Parents Keep Out!*. Buffalo, NY: Firefly Books Ltd., 2015.

WEBSITES

Intestinal Worms
embarrassingbodieskids.channel4.com/ conditions/intestinal-worms

Tapeworm
kidshealth.org/teen/infections/intestinal/ tapeworm.html

Tapeworm Infections-Causes
www.nhs.uk/Conditions/Tapeworm-infections/ Pages/Causes.aspx